Canada Close Up

Canadian Government

Elizabeth MacLeod

Scholastic Canada Ltd.
Toronto New York London Auckland Sydney
Mexico City New Delhi Hong Kong Buenos Aires

To a great Canadian, Conor
— E.M.

Scholastic Canada Ltd.
604 King Street West, Toronto, Ontario M5V 1E1, Canada

Scholastic Inc.
557 Broadway, New York, NY 10012, USA

Scholastic Australia Pty Limited
PO Box 579, Gosford, NSW 2250, Australia

Scholastic New Zealand Limited
Private Bag 94407, Botany, Manukau 2163, New Zealand

Scholastic Children's Books
Euston House, 24 Eversholt Street, London NW1 1DB, UK

www.scholastic.ca

Library and Archives Canada Cataloguing in Publication
MacLeod, Elizabeth
Canadian government / Elizabeth MacLeod.

(Canada close up)
ISBN 978-1-4431-1965-8

1. Canada--Politics and government--Juvenile literature.
2. Federal government--Canada. I. Title. II. Series: Canada
close up (Toronto, Ont.)

JL75.M23 2013   j320.471   C2012-905325-2

6 5 4 3 2 1   Printed in Canada 119   13 14 15 16 17

Table of Contents

Pronunciation Guide
a as in cat; ah as in call; ee as in see; eh as in pet;
i as in pit; oh as in ocean; oo as in food; ur as in fur;
uh as in but

Governments Across Canada

You may think **government** doesn't affect you much. But government decides many things, such as how much money to spend on health care or whether to join a war. It even decides how many dogs your family can own, what you learn in school and much more.

Canada has three levels of government: **federal** (national), **provincial** or **territorial**, and city, also known as **municipal** (myoo-NIS-uh-pul). But the most important thing about our country's government is the voters. Ordinary Canadians vote for the **politicians** who represent them at all of these levels.

Did you know that in government a cabinet isn't a place for storing dishes, it's a special group of politicians? And that pages aren't pieces of paper in a book but are young people who help the politicians? Keep reading to find out how it all works — and how you can get involved!

Chapter 1

It Happens in Ottawa

Canada is a big country but there are many things Canadians have in common. For instance, we all use the same money. The level of government that looks after issues that affect all Canadians is the federal, or country-wide, government and it's led by Canada's prime minister.

It's **election** day! All across the country, Canadians are voting. They're choosing who will represent them in Canada's federal government.

The winning candidate in each district (also called a **riding** or **constituency**) becomes a member of **Parliament** (PAHR-luh-ment), or an MP. The elected MP will go to Ottawa, Ontario, to work in the House of Commons. There, MPs gather to talk about issues, make laws and try to do what's best for the people in their riding.

The MPs belong to groups called **political parties**. Party members have similar ideas on **politics**, or how to best govern the country. For example, one party may think Canadians should pay more taxes, while another wants lower taxes. Or one party calls for a larger army, while another doesn't want to focus on the military.

Canada's federal government has five main political parties:

- Liberal (Grits)
- Conservative (Tories)
- New Democratic Party (NDP)
- Green (The Greens)
- Bloc Québécois (also known as the Bloc)

The party that elects the most candidates in the federal election forms Canada's government. The party leader becomes the prime minister, or PM, the leader of the country. The party with the second-largest number of votes is the official Opposition.

Working closely with the prime minister are a group of about 30 experienced MPs from his party who advise him. They are known as the **cabinet**. Most cabinet members look after a particular government department, such as defence, the environment or finance. Together, the prime minister and cabinet form a part of government called the **executive** branch.

Canada's federal government has three branches. The job of the executive branch is to propose **bills**. The **legislative** (LEHYJ-is-lay-tiv) branch — the House of Commons and the Senate — debates these bills and votes on them. These two branches are called Parliament.

The third branch, the **judicial** (joo-DISH-uhl) branch, is the courts. It takes the laws that Parliament passes and decides exactly what they mean and how they apply to Canadians.

How does it all work? Soon after the election, the prime minister, cabinet and other elected MPs gather in the House of Commons. There, they begin proposing and passing bills. More than half the MPs need to vote for a bill for it to be approved.

If the prime minister's party won more than half the seats in the House of Commons, it has a majority government. MPs in the same party will usually vote

Canada's Government

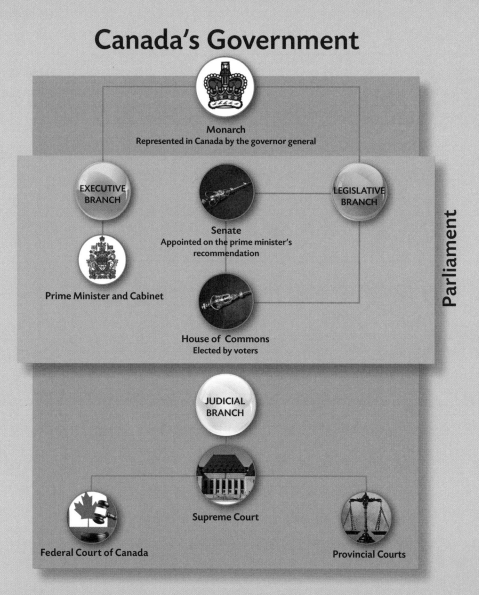

Monarch
Represented in Canada by the governor general

EXECUTIVE
BRANCH

LEGISLATIVE
BRANCH

Senate
Appointed on the prime minister's
recommendation

Prime Minister and Cabinet

House of Commons
Elected by voters

Parliament

JUDICIAL
BRANCH

Supreme Court

Federal Court of Canada

Provincial Courts

the same way and the bill will pass. If the prime minister's party only has a minority — more seats than any other party, but less than half — then they will have to get MPs from other parties to vote for the bill. It can be harder to get a bill passed.

After a bill is discussed, voted on and passed in the House of Commons, it moves on to a second part of Parliament called the Senate (SEHN-it). There are about 100 senators who meet in the Senate.

The senators come from all regions of the country and each was appointed by a prime minister. Their job is to take a careful second look at any bills that the House of Commons has approved.

Senators bring many different experiences to their work. For instance, Senator Nancy Greene Raine was an Olympic skier and Tommy Banks was a musician. Anne Cools was the first black Canadian in the Senate and Roméo Dallaire was an army general.

Some people think senators should be elected by Canadians, not appointed by the prime minister. Since the Senate hardly ever rejects bills that the House of Commons has passed, some Canadians believe the Senate should be eliminated.

Even after the Senate passes a bill, it's still not ready to become a law. One more person, the governor general, has to approve it.

The Senate (above) is known as the "Red Chamber," while the House of Commons is called the "Green Chamber." Can you see why?

The Queen with Prime Minister Harper, at a Canada Day celebration.

The governor general represents Canada's monarch, who is also the king or queen of the United Kingdom and other countries. Canada is a **constitutional monarchy** (MAHN-are-kee), which means that the monarch's powers are limited by Canada's **constitution**, or basic laws. The monarch can't always be in Canada to approve bills so she is represented by the governor general (see chapter 4). Once the governor general approves the bill, it is finally a law.

The judicial branch then interprets and applies the laws that Parliament passes.

The highest court in Canada is called the Supreme Court. It decides if laws agree with Canada's constitution. If Canadians wish to dispute a decision made by another court, they can take the case before the nine judges of the Supreme Court. One of the most important things the Supreme Court does is make sure the legislative and executive branches don't become too powerful. It's important that Parliament always keep in mind that it serves Canadian voters. The judicial branch also includes federal courts of law.

Sometimes a prime minister or premier will prorogue, or suspend, Parliament. No elections are held and the top party stays in power. Bills that are being discussed have to be reintroduced when Parliament meets again, days or months later. Many people think proroguing is unfair. It stops discussion of controversial issues. Leaders tend to prorogue Parliament when they think their government might be defeated.

Why does the federal government need to create bills? This level of government has to make a lot of decisions that affect all Canadians. For instance, the federal government controls Canadian banks as well as our system of money. It also gives money and assistance to people who need help. These may be people who can't find jobs. Or they may be seniors or disabled people who have extra expenses.

What else? The federal government meets with the Assembly of First Nations (see page 16) and helps develop northern

Federal politicians make decisions about how big the armed forces should be.

Canada. It also collects information about Canadians every few years with a **census** and uses the information to help govern the country. When you mail a letter or package, you're using a federal government service. And it's this level of government that issues patents on new inventions. Some prisons across the country are run by the federal government.

Providing so many services for Canadians costs a lot of money. The main way the federal government raises money is by collecting **taxes**. Most people who have jobs pay tax on the amount of money they earn. When you buy something, you pay tax based on how much it costs.

The federal government meets with other countries to discuss how to work together. It also decides who can immigrate to Canada, or come from other countries to live here.

Politicians Who Helped Build Canada

The Fathers of Confederation

It was a conference held in Charlottetown, Prince Edward Island, that really started talk of a united country of Canada. The Maritime provinces of Nova Scotia, New Brunswick and PEI had been talking about joining  together. So their representatives made plans to meet in September 1864. Politicians from Canada West and Canada East (now Ontario and Quebec) asked to attend so they could all talk about an even larger union. Other conferences followed, like the one held in 1886 in London, England (shown above). **Confederation** became official on July 1, 1867. The new country, the Dominion of Canada, consisted of Ontario and Quebec, New Brunswick and Nova Scotia. PEI joined in 1873.

PM Firsts

Sir John A. Macdonald had worked hard to unite Canada West, Canada East and Maritime provinces into a strong country. No wonder that when the Dominion of Canada was formed, Macdonald became its first prime minister. The first Canadian–born PM was Sir John Abbott (the third PM). The first French–Canadian PM was Sir Wilfrid Laurier (the seventh PM). Kim Campbell, the nineteenth PM, was the first woman.

Joey Smallwood

In the early 1900s, Joey Smallwood grew up in extreme poverty in Newfoundland. When he was older, he was convinced his island home should become part of Canada. This strong-willed, courageous politician brought Newfoundland into Confederation in 1949. Smallwood became the new province's first **premier** (PREEM-year), a position he held for nearly 25 years.

Leading a New Territory

Nunavut was declared a territory on April 1, 1999. Paul Okalik (below), the first Inuk lawyer in the Northwest Territories and Nunavut, became the first premier of the new territory. It was a tough job. Nunavut is a vast region with a lot of unemployment. Okalik had to organize the territory's government in a way that reflects traditional Inuit knowledge and values.

The Assembly of First Nations (AFN) is the political organization that represents First Nations people across Canada. There are more than 600 First Nation communities in Canada that are members of the AFN. Each of those communities, or bands, has a Chief and band council. These Chiefs represent their communities at the AFN.

This organization works to protect the rights of First Nations people in Canada. For many years, Aboriginal people weren't allowed to speak their own languages or practice their traditional religions. The AFN has fought discrimination and improved health care, education and more for Aboriginal people.

Today, new issues concern the AFN. Valuable resources, such as minerals, oil and natural gas, have been found on First Nations land. The communities want to develop these resources to earn money from them. But the First Nations people also know that this must be done carefully to protect the environment.

Even if you don't want to be a politician, judge or government employee (civil servant) when you're older, there are many ways to get involved in the federal government.

A tour group takes in Confederation Hall, in the House of Commons.

When you're a university student you can work as a page in the House of Commons or Senate. Pages deliver messages to the MPs, hand out official documents and more.

Members of the public can tour the Parliament Buildings and watch politics in action. If you were to attend a House of Commons debate, you might be surprised. MPs have strong feelings about issues and when they get excited, they may start yelling. The **Speaker** of the House is the person who tries to control the debate.

The House of Commons mace.

Every meeting of MPs in the House of Commons — it's called a "sitting" — starts with the Speaker sitting in his special chair. Then the Sergeant-at-Arms puts the mace in front of the Speaker. The mace is a big, gold-plated club that represents the House's power. The Speaker says a prayer, then the sitting really gets started.

The prime minister and experienced politicians sit in the front seats in the House. The newer MPs sit farther back, so they are known as "backbenchers."

The noisiest part of a sitting is Question Period. That's when opposition MPs debate the government about bills that the government wants to pass.

When MPs aren't in the House, they're often working on one of the many committees, such as the Health Committee or the Fisheries and Oceans Committee. Back home, they meet with people in their constituencies and try to deal with any concerns they have.

MPs and senators represent Canadians from every province and territory. Their numbers vary depending on many things, including the size of the province. Here is the breakdown for the 41st Parliament:

Province/Territory	MPs	Senators
Alberta	28	6
British Columbia	36	5
Manitoba	14	6
New Brunswick	10	10
Newfoundland & Labrador	7	5
Northwest Territories	1	1
Nova Scotia	11	10
Nunavut	1	1
Ontario	106	23
Prince Edward Island	4	4
Quebec	75	24
Saskatchewan	14	5
Yukon	1	1
Vacant seats*		4
TOTAL	**308**	**105**

*There are vacant seats in the House of Commons or Senate when, for instance, MPs or senators have died or resigned and have not yet been replaced.

The House of Commons and the Senate are located in the Parliament Buildings. Overlooking the Ottawa River, they're on a hill that's often known as Parliament Hill or just "the Hill."

The Parliament Buildings are made up of three buildings. The largest one is called the Centre Block, because it's in the middle of the area. It contains the Commons and Senate chambers, as well as the round Library of Parliament at the back and the tall Peace Tower at the front. This tower includes a large clock and 53 bells that are played frequently.

The buildings on either side of the Centre Block are called the East Block and the West Block. Senators and members of Parliament have their offices here.

What else can you find on the Hill? Cats! At one time cats were used to control mice in the Parliament Buildings. Now a small colony of felines lives in an area on the Hill called the Cat Sanctuary. Volunteers feed and care for them.

A view of the Parliament Buildings, showing the tall Peace Tower and the round Library of Parliament.

There are statues of famous people, including former prime ministers, the Famous Five (see page 32), Queen Elizabeth II and more on the grounds around the buildings. You can see many other monuments here too, including the Centennial Flame. It was first lit in 1967 by Prime Minister Lester B. Pearson to mark Canada's first one hundred years as a country.

Chapter 2

In the Provinces and Territories

Some provinces are surrounded by water and need laws about fishing and shipping. Others have mines and need rules to keep them safe for workers. Each Canadian province and territory has its own requirements and issues. That's why provincial and territorial governments have been set up to help Canadians in each different region.

Canada's provincial and territorial governments are similar to the federal government in many ways. Each has a chamber where bills and other issues are discussed. In the federal government, it's called the House of Commons, while in most provinces, it's known as the legislative assembly. Provincial **legislatures** have a Speaker, as in the House of Commons, to help keep order. In both cases, the Speaker is elected by the members.

In most provinces and territories, the legislature is called the Legislative Assembly and the people who represent the voters are members of the Legislative Assembly (MLAs). But in Nova Scotia and Newfoundland and Labrador, the legislature is known as the House of Assembly, and in Newfoundland the elected politicians are members of the House of Assembly (MHAs). In Ontario, the politicians are known as members of the Provincial Parliament (MPPs). The legislature in Quebec is called the National Assembly and the politicians are members of the National Assembly (MNAs).

The first Legislative Assembly in Halifax, in 1758, marked the beginning of representative government in Canada.

A premier leads each province or territory's government. The premier is the leader of the party that elects the most members to the provincial legislature. Opposite the premier is the leader of the official Opposition, the party that has the second-highest number of members.

The premier has a cabinet to help make decisions. Provincial cabinets range in size from about 10 to 30 members, depending on the size of the province. Premiers try to make sure their cabinets have members to represent various parts of the province. The premier and cabinet are the executive branch of provincial government.

Governments Across Canada

The provincial and territorial legislatures meet in each region's capital city. Every legislative building has a room, or chamber, where the legislature members meet to vote on bills.

Northwest Territories
Where: **Yellowknife**
First met: **1870**
Members: **19**

Yukon
Where: **Whitehorse**
First met: **1900**
Members: **19**

British Columbia
Where: **Victoria**
First met: **1871**
Members: **85**

Alberta
Where: **Edmonton**
First met: **1906**
Members: **87**

Saskatchewan
Where: **Regina**
First met: **1906**
Members: **58**

Manitoba
Where: **Winnipeg**
First met: **1871**
Members: **57**

Nunavut
Where: **Iqaluit**
First met: **1999**
Members: **19**

Newfoundland and Labrador
Where: **St. John's**
First met: **1833**
Members: **48**

Prince Edward Island
Where: **Charlottetown**
First met: **1773**
Members: **27**

Nova Scotia
Where: **Halifax**
First met: **1758**
Members: **52**

Ontario
Where: **Toronto**
First met: **1867**
Members: **107**

Quebec
Where: **Quebec City**
First met: **1867**
Members: **125**

New Brunswick
Where: **Fredericton**
First met: **1786**
Members: **55**

Political parties are similar at the federal and provincial or territorial level. For instance, most provinces have Conservative, Green, Liberal and NDP parties. The Bloc Québécois is a federal party but the provincial Parti Québécois is similar to it. Other special provincial parties include Alberta's Wildrose party and the Saskatchewan Party.

Instead of a governor general, each province has a lieutenant (lef-TEN-ant) governor. He is recommended by the prime minister, with advice from the province's premier, then appointed by Canada's governor general. Like the governor general, the lieutenant governor represents the king or queen in Canada. The three territories each have a commissioner, with tasks similar to a lieutenant governor's.

As in the House of Commons, the provincial government presents bills to the legislature and the members vote on them. There is no Senate at the provincial level. The lieutenant governor or commissioner gives the bill "royal assent," which means she approves it, and then it becomes law.

Like the federal government, provincial governments are responsible for some laws and prisons. Provincial governments also look after developing natural resources and protecting the environment. They are responsible for hospitals and schools.

To help pay for all of these services, the provinces and territories receive **transfer payments** from the federal government. Some regions receive more money than others. Every province except Alberta charges a provincial sales tax on most items that you buy. The territories don't charge their citizens sales tax. It already costs a lot to live there because of the high cost of flying in food and other items.

Provincial and territorial governments are responsible for schools.

The territories operate a little differently from the provinces. In the Northwest Territories and Nunavut, legislative members are not elected from political parties. All members in each territory vote to choose one of their fellow members to be the territory's premier. The members discuss issues and cooperate to make decisions on which all members agree.

The federal government has more control over the territories. It looks after natural resources and taxes there. Since the federal government owns the land in the territories, it also deals with claims by First Nations about what land belongs to them. Provincial and territorial governments have a judicial branch, just as the federal government does. There can be several levels of courts, including one to deal with traffic tickets or ones for cases about small amounts of money (small claims courts). Other courts, called superior courts, handle more serious cases.

Perhaps one of the most important things that provincial and territorial governments do is set up and help the third level of government — at the municipal level (see chapter 3).

Did you know that Canadian women weren't able to vote in federal elections until 1918? Women had to fight for the right to cast a ballot, as shown in this 1914 cartoon from the women's page of a Canadian farming journal.

Find out when women first voted in elections in your province or territory:

1916   Manitoba, Saskatchewan, Alberta
1917   British Columbia, Ontario
1918   Nova Scotia
1919   New Brunswick, Yukon
1922   Prince Edward Island
1925   Newfoundland and Labrador
1940   Quebec
1951   Northwest Territories
         (Nunavut was part of NWT until 1999)

The Famous Five

Today Canadians take for granted women's right to be MPs and senators. But these rights are thanks to a group of women known as the Famous Five: Henrietta Muir Edwards, Nellie McClung, Louise McKinney, Emily Murphy and Irene Parlby. The women joined together when Murphy was told she couldn't be a magistrate (MAJ-uh-streyt), a type of judge, because according to Canadian laws, she, like all women, wasn't a person. In 1927 the Famous Five sent a petition to the Supreme Court of Canada challenging this ruling. But they were told again women weren't persons. So the women appealed to the Privy Council of England, then Canada's highest court. In 1929, it ruled women were persons. Thanks to the Famous Five, women could now hold any government office.

Thérèse Casgrain

In 1912, Thérèse Casgrain's family just missed sailing on the *Titanic*'s tragic voyage. That was lucky for them — and, later, for female voters in Quebec, who had been fighting for the right to vote for years. In 1940, Casgrain helped them win. In 1951, she became the first woman to lead a political party in Quebec when she was elected head of the Quebec wing of the Co-Operative Commonwealth Federation party.

Rosemary Brown

When Rosemary Brown came to Canada from Jamaica in 1950, she found it tough to get a job or a place to live because she was black. So Brown vowed to make changes. In 1972, she was elected to British Columbia's legislature — and became the first black woman elected in Canadian politics.

Nellie Cournoyea

By the time Nellie Cournoyea was eight, she was interested in politics and had the job of recording what was said at her community's meetings in the Northwest Territories. Cournoyea was elected to lead the NWT in 1991. That made her the first Aboriginal woman elected premier, in a territory one-fifth the size of all of Canada!

Chapter 3

Government on Your Street

Canada's third level of government is municipal, or city, government. This level manages things that affect individual cities, towns and villages. Voters elect a councillor (or alderman) to represent their district or **ward**. They also elect a mayor (sometimes called a reeve or warden). Canada has about 4,000 municipal governments.

Municipal governments arrange for your garbage pick-up and recycling.

Of Canada's three levels of government, municipal government is the one that affects you most often. It's this level of government that makes sure your home gets electricity and water. Municipal governments also look after local libraries, sewage and licensing pets.

Your municipal government provides emergency services, such as ambulances, firefighters and police. City governments are also responsible for public transportation, including subways in larger cities. As well, they must build and maintain roads and sidewalks.

What else? Municipal governments plan how land in their communities will be used — will homes be built there? What about factories? Where should a park be placed?

Your city government oversees the parks in your neighbourhood.

This level of government helps businesses develop and grow. It makes building companies get permits so their buildings are properly constructed. Some municipal governments support local arts programs.

The province or territory sets up municipal governments, decides what powers they will have and makes rules about elections, responsibilities and more.

Just like Canada's federal government, the country's municipal government is based on the British system of government, with councils and mayors.

Voters in each municipality elect councillors (sometimes called aldermen) to represent them. The smaller districts in a municipality are called wards. Areas that don't have a lot of people living in them are organized into counties or regions, rather than wards.

The councillors from all of the wards gather together in a group called a council. It's led by a mayor in most cities. The head of the council in some villages and rural municipalities is called a reeve. In Quebec and the Maritimes, a county council is led by a warden. What is the leader called where you live?

Some of the most important work the mayor and council do is pass rules, called **by-laws**, and make sure that people follow them. These by-laws cover everything from parking and noisy neighbours to how quickly people have to clear their sidewalks after a snowstorm and keeping construction workers safe.

Edmonton has one of Canada's most unique and modern city halls.

Usually the government of the province or territory where the municipality is located also has to approve the city's by-laws.

It's expensive for municipalities to provide so many services. So the municipal governments charge people taxes depending on how much property they own. Municipalities also raise money by requiring people to pay for permits and licences, as well as collecting fines when people don't obey the by-laws.

In Toronto, the municipal government provides public transit, such as streetcars, to help people get around.

A big chunk of the money that municipalities spend comes from the federal and provincial or territorial governments. The two larger levels of government give municipalities grants known as transfer payments. For instance, Transport Canada, a federal transportation department, helps cities and towns build airports, harbours and railways.

Some communities are too small to have their own police forces. Their policing is provided by the Royal Canadian Mounted Police or provincial forces. The federal government also gives municipalities money to develop arts activities and run social programs for kids and disabled and impoverished people.

One big difference from the other levels of government is that there are no political parties in city politics. Municipal councillors are known as independents. They don't belong to any political parties, such as the Conservatives or NDP.

Perhaps because there are no political parties competing against each other, Canadians don't get very excited about municipal elections. Voter turnout can be very low, even though municipal government is the level that affects people's day-to-day lives more than any other.

If you want to find out more about municipal government or you have a question about the services your city provides, send an e-mail to your councillor or alderman or look at his or her website.

Toronto, Ontario, is Canada's largest municipality, with about 2.5 million residents and 44 wards. (Most municipalities have between 5 and 20 wards.) Greenwood, British Columbia, is the country's smallest city and has only about 600 citizens.

Politicians Who Represent Canada's Diversity

Louis Robichaud

Louis Robichaud became the first Acadian elected premier of New Brunswick in 1960. Acadians are descendants of colonists from France who settled in the Maritimes during the 1600s in an area known as Acadia. Robichaud was proud of his Acadian heritage and under his administration, New Brunswick became Canada's only officially bilingual province. As a senator, he supported bilingualism and national unity.

Lincoln Alexander

In 1968, Lincoln Alexander became the first black Canadian elected to the House of Commons. He was named Ontario's lieutenant governor in 1985. Once again, he was the first person of colour to hold this position. Multiculturalism was always important to Alexander, as were education and youth issues.

Steven Fletcher

Steven Fletcher is a member of Parliament and a health care activist. He was in a car accident at the age of 23, which left him paralyzed from the neck down. This Manitoban politician became Canada's first physically disabled MP in 2004. In the House of Commons, an aide helps Fletcher turn pages and lets the Speaker know when he needs to speak or vote.

Roberta Jamieson

A dynamic Mohawk leader, Roberta Jamieson's life includes many firsts. In 1976 she became the first First Nations woman in Canada to become a lawyer. Then in

2001, she became the first female Chief of the Six Nations of the Grand River reserve in Ontario. A passionate risk-taker, Jamieson works hard for better relations between government and First Nations people.

Naheed Nenshi

When Naheed Nenshi decided to run for mayor of Calgary, Alberta in 2010, he seemed like a long shot to win. But Nenshi used Facebook, Twitter and YouTube to tell people about his plans and involve voters. Using social media worked to get his message out, especially with young voters. Nenshi was elected mayor — the first Muslim to be elected mayor of a major Canadian city.

Chapter 4

Canada's Governors General

Canada's prime minister is the head of government, but the official head of State is the king or queen of Canada. Representing the monarch in Canada is the governor general. There have been more than 25 governors general in Canada since Confederation. They have all lived at Rideau (REE-doh) Hall, in Ottawa.

The governor general represents Canada around the world. Here, Governor General Michaëlle Jean speaks with school children on a visit to Haiti.

Canadians don't elect their governor general. Instead, the prime minister selects someone. He tells the monarch, who then appoints that person. The governor general works with the members of the House of Commons and Senate. When it's time for an election, the prime minister asks the governor general for permission, and the prime minister then makes an announcement to all Canadians.

After an election, when the House of Commons first meets again, the governor general reads out the government's Speech from the Throne. It's written by the party in power and describes what it plans to do in the next session, or term, of Parliament. The governor general also swears in the cabinet ministers.

After the members of the House of Commons and the Senate vote on and approve a bill, the governor general must sign the bill in a special ceremony in the Senate. This gives the bill royal assent and it becomes law.

The governor general is the Commander-in-Chief of Canada, which means she's head of the Canadian Forces. Her work also involves attending many ceremonies. As well, the governor general appoints Supreme Court justices and senators, on the prime minister's recommendation. The governor general also appoints the lieutenant governor or commissioner in each province and territory (find out more on page 28).

One of the governor general's roles is to present awards and honours that recognize outstanding Canadians. Here, Governor General David Johnston presents a Diamond Jubilee Medal to Bryden Hutt for his work supporting the Children's Wish Foundation.

Famous Governors General

First Governor General

As Governor General of British North America (Canada's name before Confederation), Charles Stanley Monck worked hard during the 1860s to pull Canada together as a united country. No wonder he was named the nation's first governor general in 1867.

First Canadian Governor General

It's hard to believe, but until 1952, no governor general had been born in Canada. Vincent Massey (right), Canada's eighteenth governor general, was born in Toronto and impressed Canadians with his hard work. This governor general travelled all over the country, sometimes by canoe or dog team!

First Female Governor General

When Jeanne Sauvé become Canada's first female governor general in 1984, she'd already achieved many firsts, including being the first female Speaker of the House of Commons. As governor general, she focused on national unity, peace and youth. Canada has had two more female governors general: Adrienne Clarkson and Michaëlle Jean.

Governor General's Literary Awards

John Buchan, also known as Lord Tweedsmuir, was not only Canada's fifteenth governor general but was a bestselling writer as well. He helped start the Governor General's Literary Awards in 1936. Some of Canada's best books have won this award!

Sporty Governors General

Sports wouldn't be the same without Canada's governors general. The Grey Cup, Canadian football's top award, was created by the ninth governor general, Earl Grey. Other governors general have donated trophies for sports ranging from lacrosse and dragon boat racing to ringette and fishing. Lord Stanley, the sixth governor general, donated hockey's Stanley Cup, the oldest trophy for pro athletes in North America. It is shown here in front of the first Stanley Cup champions, the Montreal AAA hockey team, in 1893.

Chapter 5

Getting Involved and Voting

Most Canadians never become prime ministers, premiers or mayors. However there's a more important way they can participate in government — by getting involved and voting. You have to be eighteen years old to vote in Canada but you can begin to participate at any age.

Canada is a **democracy** (di-MOCK-ruh-see), which means Canadians can vote and choose whom they want for their leaders. No one can just declare himself prime minister or mayor — he has to win an election. If Canadians don't like how the people they've elected do their jobs, those people likely won't win the next election.

On election day in Canada, voters go to a **polling station** in their riding. There, they show identification and proof of address, then their names are checked off the voters' list. That ensures that no one votes more than once. Next, voters are given a piece of paper listing the name of every person, or candidate, running in the election. This paper is called a ballot.

In a democracy, people vote on issues that affect them. If Canadians personally voted on every government issue, Canada's system of government would be known as direct democracy. That's not practical in a big country like Canada. Instead, Canadians vote for politicians to represent their views — it's called representative democracy.

It's probably not a secret who Prime Minister Harper voted for.

Voters take the ballot to a private voting booth, and mark an "X" beside the candidate they want to elect. Voters then fold their ballots and the ballots go into a box. No one knows who any voter chooses, and nobody can force another person to vote a particular way.

When the voting time is over, the polling station closes and the votes are counted. As computer technology improves, you may one day be able to vote on-line but it's not a secure enough way to vote yet.

Politicians Who Left a Lasting Legacy

Tommy Douglas
When Tommy Douglas was seven, in 1911, he needed surgery but his parents couldn't afford it. Luckily, a doctor agreed to operate for free. Douglas never forgot. He became a member of Parliament representing Saskatchewan, as well as the province's premier, and the first leader of the federal New Democratic Party. In 1962, Douglas's work helped bring in Medicare, a program providing medical care for all Canadians.

Lester B. Pearson
Canadians have Lester B. Pearson to thank for our red-and-white maple leaf flag. He was prime minister in 1965 when MPs voted in favour of a unique flag for Canada. He is shown here, in 1964, holding up the winning design of Canada's new flag. Before that, in 1957, Ontario-born Pearson won the Nobel Peace Prize, making him the only Canadian to win this award.

Pierre Trudeau

Trudeau was prime minister in the 1970s and early 1980s. His style inspired young Canadians and caused "Trudeaumania." Fans liked his push for bilingualism and multiculturalism. During the 1970's October Crisis, Trudeau stood up to the Front de libération de Québec (FLQ) terrorists. He is shown here in 1982, sitting with Queen Elizabeth II as she signs the Constitution Act. Thanks to Trudeau, changes to Canada's constitution (basic rules and laws) are now made in Canada, not Britain. But Trudeau was not popular with everyone. His 1980 National Energy Policy made many Westerners feel cheated. In Quebec some people disliked his stand against the province's separation.

Although you have to be 18 years old to vote in actual elections, you can find out what it's like to vote by taking part in a program like Student Vote. Your results can't count in the real election, but you'll discover what it's like to listen to the candidates, consider what they have to say and finally mark a ballot. Student Vote is free and any school can join up.

How else can you get involved with Canada's government? Find out about the political parties. You can send politicians questions about issues that matter to you. You can also get involved in your school's government.

You can have fun and learn a lot when you get involved in elections.

When Ellen Fairclough ran for council in Hamilton, Ontario, in 1945, she lost — by just three votes. "No one can ever tell me," she said, "that a single vote does not count!" Eventually Fairclough was elected to council, and later to federal politics. She was even appointed to the cabinet.

Many people who are able to vote don't bother. In the 2008 federal election, less than 60% of Canadians voted. Too busy, forgot, sick, think the candidates are all the same — those are just some of the excuses they gave. But the main reason is that they're not interested.

Governments need to make people realize how important their votes are. In about 30 countries around the world, citizens must vote or pay a fine. Perhaps more Canadians will vote in future if they're able to do it on-line since it will be fast and easy.

If you start voting when you're a teenager, you're likely to vote for the rest of your life. You may even end up running in an election for Canada's government!

Glossary

Bills: suggestions for laws that the government would like to make to help govern Canada

By-laws: local community laws or rules

Cabinet: advisors to the prime minister or premier

Census: an official count of the number of people in an area (may include details such as people's ages, jobs and more)

Confederation: the uniting of provinces in 1867 to form the country of Canada

Constituency: a district or riding that elects a politician to represent it in federal or provincial government

Constitution: a country's highest rules and laws

Constitutional monarchy: a country that has a monarch, but the monarch's powers are limited by the country's constitution

Democracy: a type of government in which the people who will be governed choose the people in the government through voting

Election: the selecting of a person by voting

Executive branch: the part of government that makes sure laws and plans are carried out

Federal: national or country-wide

Government: the system by which a country, province, territory or city is directed or ruled

Judicial branch: the part of government that interprets and applies laws

Legislative branch: the part of government that makes new laws and changes or removes old laws

Legislature: a gathering of elected members of Parliament who have the power to pass, change and cancel laws. In Canada, there is a federal legislature (Parliament), as well as provincial and territorial legislatures.

Municipal: belonging to, or associated with, a city or town

Parliament: a federal or provincial/territorial legislature. In the federal government, it is divided into the House of Commons and the Senate.

Political party: people who share similar ideas about how to govern a country or province

Politician: a person involved in politics

Politics: running government and making decisions about officials and policies

Polling station: a place where people go in an election to vote

Premier: the head of a provincial or territorial government

Provincial: belonging to, or associated with, one of Canada's ten provinces

Riding: a voting region or constituency

Speaker: the person who directs debates in federal and provincial/territorial parliaments

Taxes: money people pay to the government to provide facilities and services

Territorial: belonging to, or associated with, one of Canada's three territories

Transfer payments: payments from a government to other governments (for example for Medicare, colleges and university) or to individual people (including family allowances and old-age pensions)

Ward: a municipal district represented by a councillor

Index

Acknowledgements

Special thanks to Stacy Gilchrist for her support and generosity. Thank you to the office of the Governor General of Canada and the Office of the Lieutenant Governor of Ontario. Many thanks to everyone at Scholastic Canada, especially Anne Shone, a most excellent and democratic editor! Special thanks also to art director Andrea Casault and the French translators at Éditions Scholastic.
Love always to Paul — so glad I joined your party.

Photo Credits

Front cover (flags): zennie/iStockphoto.com; (Parliament buildings): Rambleon/ Shutterstock.com; (ballot box): Elections Canada; back cover: Mahesh Patil/ Shutterstock.com; page iv: Student Vote; 2: Rambleon/Shutterstock.com; 3: AK2/iStock, used with the permission of the Bank of Canada; 4: Elections Canada; 7 (coat of arms): Koshevnyk/Shutterstock.com; 7 (Senate mace): MAC-009 © Library of Parliament/ Gordon King; 7 and 18 (House of Commons mace): MAC-003 © Library of Parliament/ Mone Cheng; 7 (Supreme Court): aiok/Shutterstock.com; 7 (gavel): Andrey Burmakin/ Shutterstock.com; 7 (scales): MilousSK/Shutterstock.com; 9 (Senate): SEN-41st-Parl. © Library of Parliament/Marc Fowler; 9 (House of Commons): HOC-41st_Parl © Library of Parliament/Roy Grogan; 10: The Canadian Press/Adrian Wyld; 12: Vince Talotta/GetStock.com; 14: C-149461/Library and Archives Canada; 15: The Canadian Press/Kevin Frayer; 17: PIO-133 © Library of Parliament/Roy Grogan; 21: intoit/ Shutterstock.com; 22: Jeff Whyte/Shutterstock.com; 23: Mary Lane/Shutterstock.com; 25: C-013955/Library and Archives Canada; 26: Joe Iera/Shutterstock.com; 29: dotshock/Shutterstock.com; 31: NA-3818-14/Glenbow Archives; 32: Images Etc. Ltd./GetStock.com; 34: Denis Roger/Shutterstock.com; 35: City of Toronto; 36: imageegami/Shutterstock.com; 37: David P. Lewis/Shutterstock.com; 39: Richard Cummins/Corbis; 40: GVictoria/Shutterstock.com; 42: Office of the Lieutenant Governor of Ontario; 43 (upper): Steve Russell/GetStock.com; 43: Office of the Mayor, The City of Calgary; 44: The Canadian Press/Fred Chartrand; 45: rook76/ Shutterstock.com, Courtesy Canada Post 2002; 46: The Canadian Press/Tom Hanson; 47: The Canadian Press/Sean Kilpatrock; 48: e002265642/Library and Archives Canada; 49: Hockey Hall of Fame; 50: Student Vote; 51: tele52/Shutterstock.com; Tony Bock/Toronto Star/GetStock.com; 54: PA-13615/Library and Archives Canada/Duncan Cameron fonds/Reproduced with the permission of Library and Archives Canada; 55: Ron Bull/GetStock.com; 56: Student Vote.